STORIES FROM GRANDPA

STORIES *from* GRANDPA

A Fill-In Journal and Family Keepsake

Katie H. Sweeney

ROCKRIDGE
PRESS

Interior and Cover Designer: Lindsey Dekker
Art Producer: Michael Hardgrove
Editor: Arturo Conde
Production Editor: Nora Millman
Interior art used under license from © Creativemarket.com & Shutterstock.com.
Author photo courtesy of © Jasmin Van T Photography

ISBN: 978-1-64739-612-1
R0

This journal belongs to:

_____

Contents

Introduction

Why You Need to Tell Your Story

As a grandfather, you have an important story to tell. Hearing your unique memories and interesting perspectives not only helps the younger generation better understand their origin, but also guides them on their own life's journey. The only problem is that, with so many life experiences to recount, it's difficult to know where to begin or how to articulate the lessons you'd like to pass down to your children and grandchildren.

Luckily, you've picked up this book. *Stories from Grandpa* is a journal meant to help you share your life's narrative with your grandchildren. The details you'll be prompted to describe on each page will give family members a glimpse into where you came from, what you experienced in your life, and what you hope for the future. It's time to think about your feelings, record likes and dislikes, and discover new dreams and wishes. Now is your chance to open up and tell stories and reveal parts of yourself that your children might not even know about. It's an opportunity to describe your past and present and think about—and answer—the questions you regret not asking your own grandfather while he was alive. As you write about your own history, feelings, and thoughts, you will create a legacy that will live on long after you do. This journal will become a treasured family heirloom that will provide meaning for generations to come.

There is no right or wrong way to use this book. Open any page, read the prompt, and write as much or as little as you like. Or, start at the beginning and make your way through the chapters sequentially. You may even find it enjoyable to have a grandchild or other family member help you respond to the writing prompts. Dictate your responses while a grandchild scribbles them in

the book, or set up a video camera, have family members ask you the questions out loud, and record your answers on audio. Each chapter focuses on a different aspect of your life—from your favorite things to your professional career to the world events that shaped your outlook. The questions and activities you'll find throughout this journal are meant to trigger memories, highlight personal insights, and help you connect with the younger generations of your family.

Whether you think of your life as grand or humble, ordinary or outstanding, it is an essential part of your children's and grandchildren's heritage, and even the most seemingly mundane memories and ideas can help your loved ones navigate all the unknowns that lie ahead of them.

So just begin—and, most importantly, be yourself!

The process of journaling might surprise you and help you learn things about yourself and your life that you might not have realized before. If something comes to you that doesn't relate to a prompt or question, or you feel like you want to give a longer answer, write it down on the blank pages at the back of the book. Your thoughts, ideas, and memories will serve as inspiration to your family. By filling in these pages, you are creating a blueprint of the past that will be cherished far into the future.

CHAPTER ONE

Who You Are

Although everyone's journey from youth to old age is unique, it all begins the same: with birth. Whether you grew up in the city or the country, in a small apartment or a large house, the first few years of your life were crucial to forming who you are now. In this first chapter, start your journaling experience by sharing the most basic details about who you are. Don't know how to answer a question? Don't worry! This process is meant to be fun and rewarding. Feel free to skip prompts altogether or come back to them later if you like.

YOUR FAMILY TREE

_____
paternal grandmother

_____
paternal grandfather

_____
father

_____
mother

_____
maternal grandmother

_____
maternal grandfather

_____
sibling

_____
sibling

_____
sibling

_____
sibling

_____
sibling

_____
sibling

_____
grandchild

_____
child

_____
grandchild

_____
grandchild

_____
child

_____
grandchild

_____
grandchild

_____
child

_____
grandchild

_____
you

_____
grandchild

_____
partner

_____
child

_____
grandchild

_____
partner

_____
grandchild

_____
partner

_____
child

_____
grandchild

_____
grandchild

_____
partner

_____
child

_____
grandchild

_____
grandchild

1. What is your full name? _____

2. When is your birthday? _____

3. Where and when were you born? _____

4. What is the significance of your name? _____

   _____

   _____

5. Do you have a nickname? If so, what is it? _____

   _____

6. Who is/was (are/were) your life partner(s)? _____

   _____

7. Were you ever married? If so, what are three things you remember about getting married?

   _____

   _____

   _____

   _____

   _____

8. What are the names and birthplaces of your children?

9. What is your medical history? Have you overcome any health issues?

10. Name all the places where you have lived.

11. What five adjectives would you use to describe yourself?

CHAPTER TWO

Your Favorite Things

What things have brought you joy over the years? What items instantly put a smile on your face? What objects, places, and people, when you think about them, always cheer you up? Whatever your favorite things are—raindrops on roses, warm woolen mittens, crisp apple strudels—now is the time to share them. Write down whatever comes to mind: any of your favorite things—big, small, and every size in between. The process of identifying what makes you happy will help you get used to the idea of journaling.

What is your favorite color? Why do you love this color? Do you prefer to wear it? Decorate with it? See it in nature?

_____

_____

_____

_____

_____

What is your favorite food and/or drink?

_____

_____

_____

_____

_____

_____

What dessert do you like to have on your birthday?

What is your favorite place to visit? Why?

What is your favorite season and why?

_____

_____

_____

_____

_____

_____

What is your favorite holiday and why?

_____

_____

_____

_____

_____

_____

What are your favorite sports teams? Have they ever won a championship that seemed unwinnable?

List three of your favorite books.

Who are your favorite musical artists or groups?

_____

_____

_____

_____

_____

_____

_____

_____

List three of your favorite songs.

_____

_____

_____

What types of TV shows or movies do you like to watch?

What do you collect? Records? Artwork? Books? Why do you enjoy collecting these items?

Name three people, dead or alive, fictional or real, who you would like to have dinner with.

_____

_____

_____

If you could be an animal, which animal would you be and why?

_____

_____

_____

_____

_____

_____

_____

_____

If you could have one superpower, what would it be and why?

What makes you laugh?

Which celebrities do you find most attractive and why?

_____

_____

_____

_____

_____

Who are your role models and heroes?

_____

_____

_____

_____

_____

_____

_____

_____

What is your philosophy about life? What is your motto?

_____

_____

_____

_____

_____

_____

What are your hobbies?

_____

_____

_____

_____

_____

_____

CHAPTER THREE

Family Traditions

In this chapter, you will reflect on family memories from childhood to adulthood. The following prompts are meant to help you reminisce about the past. So take a moment to look back at your life and all that you have accomplished. If you think you haven't accomplished much, think again! You raised a family and are now a grandfather. That is something to be very proud of!

What language did you learn first? What language(s) did your parents speak? How many languages do you speak?

_____

_____

_____

_____

_____

Where are your ancestors from?

_____

_____

_____

_____

_____

What ethnicity do you identify with, and how do others identify you?

_____

_____

_____

_____

_____

What are your religious and spiritual beliefs and practices?

_____

_____

_____

_____

_____

Share a favorite story that was passed down to you from your parents, grandparents, or other family member(s).

_____

_____

_____

_____

_____

_____

Do you know any stories about the history of your family name or the origins of your family?

_____

_____

_____

_____

_____

Did your family go on vacation? If so, where? What did you do there?

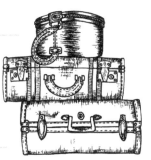

When someone passed away, how did you honor their life and memory?

In which ways are you like your parents, and in which ways are you different?

_____

_____

_____

_____

_____

_____

What are some of your important family values, and how do you put them into practice?

_____

_____

_____

_____

_____

_____

What is a tradition that you've stopped practicing but wish you could bring back? Why?

_____

_____

_____

_____

_____

_____

What traditions do you want your family to continue after you are gone?

_____

_____

_____

_____

_____

_____

_____

How do you ring in the new year—quietly at home with family or with a night out on the town? What do you eat and drink?

What food do you like to have for special family dinners?

Write down a story that you have told many times in your life but never gets old.

_____

_____

_____

_____

_____

_____

What is one ritual you've practiced your whole life and continue to do today?

_____

_____

_____

_____

_____

What is the funniest family story that you remember?

_____

_____

_____

_____

_____

_____

When you were growing up, how did your family celebrate birthdays?

_____

_____

_____

_____

_____

What holidays do you regularly celebrate? How do you celebrate them?

_____

_____

_____

_____

_____

_____

What are the qualities that you most value in a person?

_____

_____

_____

_____

_____

_____

CHAPTER FOUR

Growing Up

Although it's probably been a long time since you were a child, there are most likely plenty of things you remember about your life as a little kid. Maybe you remember the order that you picked up from the butcher every week for your mother or the songs that you sang with the high school choir or the name of the shoe store where you and your older sister worked. Whatever comes to mind, jot it down. Return to your childhood home in your mind and see if you can recall what your day-to-day life was like back then.

What do you remember most about your mother?

What do you remember most about your father?

What were your parents' occupations? Did they enjoy their work?

What do you remember most about your grandparents?

Which family member were you closest to? What makes you feel closest to them?

_____

_____

_____

_____

_____

_____

What was your childhood like?

_____

_____

_____

_____

What did you enjoy doing as a teen?

What hardships did you overcome as a child or teenager?

Did you ever get into trouble as a teenager? What happened?

_____

_____

_____

_____

_____

Describe your first kiss.

_____

_____

_____

_____

_____

Did you have a pet? If so, what kind of animal was it and what was its name?

_____

_____

_____

_____

_____

_____

What types of chores did you do as a child?

_____

_____

_____

_____

_____

Did you get an allowance? How much was it?

Describe a typical day in your childhood.

What games did you like to play when you were young?

_____

_____

_____

_____

_____

_____

What did your first home look like?

_____

_____

_____

_____

_____

_____

_____

Who lived in your childhood home?

Did you have your own bedroom? Describe your space.

Do you know how much your parents paid for rent or mortgage?

Did you learn how to drive? If so, who taught you, and what do you remember about the experience? If not, how did you get from one place to another?

CHAPTER FIVE

School Days and Life Lessons

Whether you didn't get past the eighth grade or have a graduate degree from a prestigious university, you've learned many things throughout your life. You certainly must know a lot! Here is your chance to share your wisdom with the generations to come. If these questions seem tough to answer, take a deep breath: Your perspective, experience, and advice matter. Don't be afraid to share things that your family might not know about you. There is no time like the present to reveal something extraordinary about your past.

Where did you go to school? Write a list of all of the schools you attended (or the ones you remember), from preschool to graduate programs.

_____

_____

_____

_____

_____

_____

What was a valuable life lesson you learned, in or out of the classroom?

_____

_____

_____

_____

_____

_____

What type of student were you? Did you get good grades or barely pass? Did you enjoy homework or hate it?

_____

_____

_____

_____

_____

What were your best and worst subjects in school?

_____

_____

_____

_____

_____

_____

_____

Did you play any sports or instruments or participate in school activities? What did you enjoy?

_____

_____

_____

_____

_____

_____

If you could enroll in a university or college today, what would you study?

_____

_____

_____

_____

_____

Did you have a favorite teacher or a person you looked up to who played an essential role in shaping your life?

_____

_____

_____

_____

_____

What did you want to be when you grew up?

_____

_____

_____

_____

_____

_____

What's the highest honor or award you've ever received? How did you feel about receiving the award?

_____

_____

_____

_____

_____

_____

Have you served your country in the military? When and where?

_____

_____

_____

_____

_____

_____

What's the best advice you were ever given?

Have you ever been involved in a tragic event? What happened?
What life lessons did you learn from overcoming this hardship?

Life is full of tough decisions. Describe a time when you had to make a big decision, and write about what happened afterward.

Was there any single event that drastically changed the course of your life?

What was the scariest thing you ever experienced?

_____

_____

_____

_____

_____

Describe a stressful experience that you overcame.

_____

_____

_____

_____

_____

_____

Do you have any major regrets?

_____

_____

_____

_____

_____

_____

What are some good habits that you developed early on in life?

_____

_____

_____

_____

_____

_____

What things or habits have you quit in your lifetime? Why did you quit them?

_____

_____

_____

_____

_____

_____

What is something that you would love to learn how to do?

_____

_____

_____

_____

_____

_____

CHAPTER SIX

Friends and Family

What would life be without someone to laugh with? Someone to cry with? Someone to cheer you up when you're down? Someone who finishes your sentences and celebrates your birthday? Friends and family members are important characters in your personal story. In this chapter, you'll be prompted to remember the friends who brought joy and color to your journey. Think back on the good times and bad times. Can you recall who stood by your side? Your family will enjoy reading your stories and learning more about your insights on relationships.

Who is/was your best friend, and how many years have you known or did you know each other?

_____

_____

_____

_____

_____

What do/did you like most about your best friend?

_____

_____

_____

_____

_____

_____

Who was your first love? How did you know you were in love?

Who is the greatest love of your life, and what qualities first attracted you to this person?

If you could switch places for one day with a relative or friend, who would it be and why?

When did you find out you were going to be a parent for the first time? How did you feel?

What do you enjoy most about being a father, and what do you enjoy most about being a grandfather?

_____

_____

_____

_____

How would you describe your parenting style? Looking back, is there anything that you would change?

_____

_____

_____

_____

_____

How is being a father different from being a grandfather, and vice versa?

_____

_____

_____

_____

_____

Who is your oldest friend? How long have you known each other?

_____

_____

_____

_____

_____

When, where, and how did your parents die?

_____

_____

_____

_____

_____

_____

What activities do you enjoy doing by yourself? Do you mind
spending time alone? For example, would you go to the movies or
a restaurant alone?

_____

_____

_____

_____

_____

_____

What do you talk about with your friends? What is the most important reason you stay in touch with your friends? How do you keep in contact? Do you call, exchange text messages, email, or write letters?

_____

_____

_____

_____

_____

Have you ever met a person and instantly become friends? Why do you think you connected so immediately?

_____

_____

_____

_____

Are you competitive with your friends and family? In what ways do you compete with them?

Have you ever helped a friend when they were in extreme need? What did you do for your friend, and what was the outcome?

Has a friend ever helped you when you were in desperate need? Did this change your perspective of what it means to be a friend?

_____

_____

_____

_____

_____

Is age important in a friendship? Have you ever had friends who were older or younger than you? How did the age difference affect your relationship?

_____

_____

_____

_____

_____

Are you friends with any past loves? Do you think it's possible to be friends with an ex-lover?

_____

_____

_____

_____

_____

_____

Are there any long-lost friends you wish you could reconnect with?

_____

_____

_____

_____

_____

_____

CHAPTER SEVEN

The World You Grew Up In

Y ou have lived through some monumental and memorable moments in history. In this chapter, you'll explore the major global events that have impacted your life. Maybe you experienced these happenings firsthand by fighting in a war or marching for equal rights. Perhaps you witnessed them from afar by reading about them in a paper or listening to a radio or television report. Whatever your connection is to important past events, share it. Reading your thoughts and perspectives about these pivotal life events will give your loved ones a richer understanding of history. From the moon landing to the birth of computers, no event is too big or small. If it impacted you in any way, write it down.

What are some major national and world events (such as presidential elections and historical firsts) that happened in your lifetime?

Describe one major event that happened in your past but still affects you today.

Have you lived through any significant natural disasters? What happened, and how did you survive?

What is the most life-altering innovation or event that happened during your lifetime? The nuclear bomb? The internet? A major war?

_____

_____

_____

_____

_____

What political or social cause do you support, and why?

_____

_____

_____

_____

_____

_____

What do you consider the most significant inventions of your lifetime?

_____

_____

_____

_____

_____

What do you think about modern-day technology? Love it or hate it?

_____

_____

_____

_____

_____

How would you describe today's younger generation? In what ways are they different from people in your generation?

What do you miss most about your past? Was it truly the good old days, or do you prefer the present time?

If you could change one thing about the world today, what would it be?

What do you love most about the world of today? Why?

What causes matter most to you? Health care? Shelter for the home-less? Combating corruption?

_____

_____

_____

_____

_____

What world leaders do you admire? Why?

_____

_____

_____

_____

_____

Is there any time in your life that you remember more vividly than others? What is that time and why is it so memorable?

If you had the power to solve one of the world's problems, what would it be and why?

If you won a billion dollars tomorrow, what would you do with the money?

_____

_____

_____

_____

_____

What's one thing you've always wanted but still don't have?

_____

_____

_____

_____

_____

_____

Today, society is moving to become more inclusive. Which group(s) do you think had it toughest when you were growing up?

_____

_____

_____

_____

_____

_____

What parts of modern life do you just not understand?

_____

_____

_____

_____

_____

_____

CHAPTER EIGHT

Your Job

The average person spends more than 90,000 hours (roughly ⅓ of their life) working. What you did or do professionally has played an essential part in shaping who you are. The environment in which you worked, how you worked, and who you worked with had a tremendous effect on your life. Whether you spent your time in a formal office working as the CEO of a big corporation or passed your days in a busy factory as a blue-collar worker, your career matters. Answer the following prompts to share the story of your working life with your family.

What career aspirations did you have when you were young?
What did you end up doing?

_____

_____

_____

_____

_____

What was your first job, and how much money did you earn
doing it?

_____

_____

_____

_____

_____

_____

_____

How many different jobs have you had in your lifetime? What were they? Which companies did you work for?

Of all the jobs you've had, which one did you enjoy the most and which one did you enjoy the least? Why?

Did you ever quit or get fired from a job? What happened?

_____

_____

_____

_____

_____

_____

Did you ever change career paths? Why? What career did you leave, and which one did you pursue instead?

_____

_____

_____

_____

_____

_____

What job would you like to have now if you could start over in
 your career?

_____

_____

_____

_____

_____

What was the biggest challenge you faced in your career or
working life? Did other people from your generation face the
same problem?

_____

_____

_____

_____

What kind of big and small decisions did you make throughout your career?

_____

_____

_____

_____

_____

What skills and credentials were necessary for you to perform your job to the best of your ability?

_____

_____

_____

_____

_____

Did your profession require any lifestyle changes? Did you have to travel frequently or move your family to a specific place? Did you need to work nights? Describe how these changes affected you and your family's life.

If you were a young person in today's world, do you think you would choose the same career as you did when you were younger?

What professional organizations or groups have you been a member of? What did you like and/or dislike about these groups?

_____

_____

_____

_____

_____

Describe a typical workday at the height of your career. How long was it? What did your daily agenda look like?

_____

_____

_____

_____

_____

Did you have a professional mentor? If so, who was it, and how did they help further your career?

_____

_____

_____

_____

_____

_____

_____

Were you able to retire? If so, at what age?

_____

_____

_____

_____

If you were able to retire, how have you enjoyed retirement? What have you done to pass your time?

_____

_____

_____

_____

If you were to go back to work tomorrow, what would you want to do? Why?

_____

_____

_____

_____

_____

Have you participated in any sort of community service or philan-
thropy efforts? What motivated you to give back?

How do you feel about the career choices you made? Looking back
on your professional life, would you consider it a success? Why or
why not?

CHAPTER NINE

You and Me

By now, hopefully you've gotten the hang of journaling and have developed a rhythm to answering these questions. You've talked about friends, the world you lived in, and your profession. Here you will focus on your relationship with your family. Don't shy away from your feelings. It's okay to discuss difficult things, like what you are afraid of or how hard it was to care for a sick loved one. It's also okay to talk about wonderful things, like how you've managed to find joy in each day and the big and small personal accomplishments you are especially proud of.

What do you remember about the days your children and grand-children were born? List one to three details you remember about the day each of your children and grandchildren came into the world.

What is your most treasured family memory?

Which traits do you think are the most common in your family?

How would you explain your family to a stranger?

_____

_____

_____

_____

_____

_____

What are the most challenging and most rewarding things about
growing older?

_____

_____

_____

_____

_____

What's the best gift you've ever received? Who gave it to you? The gift doesn't have to be a material possession—it could also be advice or experience.

What is your secret to happiness?

As you look back on your life, can you identify any major turning points—milestones or significant events or situations that changed the direction of your personal journey?

What can your grandchildren do to avoid having regrets later in life?

_____

_____

_____

_____

_____

_____

_____

What chores or rules did your parents give you that you chose not to impose on your children and grandchildren?

_____

_____

_____

_____

What sacrifices did you make for your family? Were the sacrifices worth it? What was the outcome?

Have you ever had to care for a sick loved one? What lessons have you learned from that experience?

What is your greatest fear for your family? What is the worst thing that could happen to your loved ones?

What could you tell your family today that they would be surprised to learn about you?

What valuable lessons did your parents or grandparents teach you that are important for the younger generations in your family to remember?

What advice do you have for your children and grandchildren about being in a committed long-term relationship or marriage?

What advice do you have for your children and grandchildren about being a parent?

What makes you proud of your children and grandchildren?

_____

_____

_____

_____

_____

_____

What's the best compliment that your children and grandchildren could give you?

_____

_____

_____

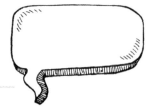

_____

Which family member do you have the most in common with today? Has that changed over time? Why?

CHAPTER TEN

Your Hopes for the Future

Congratulations! You've made it to the last chapter of this journal, and now it's time to focus on the future. Dreaming about the days to come is human nature and something that you can do at any point in life, no matter how old you may be. The following prompts will help you reflect on the past, think about how you feel in the present moment, and imagine what your future and the future of your loved ones will look like.

What haven't you done yet that you would love to do in the future? Do you have any unrealized dreams?

_____

_____

_____

_____

_____

List three things you would like to do with your family in the next six months.

_____

_____

_____

_____

_____

How do you see the world in 10 years?

_____

_____

_____

_____

_____

_____

What are your dreams for your children and grandchildren?

_____

_____

_____

_____

_____

What are your hopes for the future of the planet?

What do you see as your legacy?

In your life, what has defined you? Your experiences? Your values? The relationships you've had with loved ones? The places you have explored? Why?

_____

_____

_____

_____

_____

_____

_____

If you could go back and change something in your life, what would it be?

_____

_____

_____

_____

_____

What are your goals for the future? What do you hope to achieve in the time that is left in your life?

What do you want your family to accomplish when you are gone?

Name one way in which the world has changed to become a
better place.

What do you think will be the biggest challenge facing your
grandchildren?

What sort of things do you believe are next for humankind? Space travel? Artificial intelligence? Flying cars?

_____

_____

_____

_____

_____

If your life was made into a movie after you passed, which actor would you want to portray you? Why? What would the film focus on?

_____

_____

_____

_____

_____

Which major corporations, technologies, and gadgets will become obsolete by the time your grandchildren are your age? Why?

If you won a billion dollars the day before you die, what would you want your family to do with the money? Why?

How do you feel about death? Are you afraid of it? Why or why not?

_____

_____

_____

_____

_____

Which values (lessons from life experiences, etc.) do you hope your family will inherit from you? Honesty? Work ethic?

_____

_____

_____

_____

_____

What would you tell your grandchildren to acquire/preserve to pass down to future generations?

_____

_____

_____

_____

_____

How do you want your family to remember you?

_____

_____

_____

_____

_____

Additional Questions

Sharing memories with your family is part of a lifelong process. Now that you have created a keepsake with the fill-in journal *Stories from Grandpa*, here are more questions that you can use as prompts to create another journal or have meaningful conversations with your family. You may also consider other complementary activities like recording your answers on audio as an additional keepsake that your family will cherish for generations to come.

What sort of things or activities bring you joy? When are you most happy?

_____

_____

_____

_____

_____

What's the most fantastic thing that's happened in your life?

_____

_____

_____

_____

_____

Many believe that age is just a number. What age do you feel you are? Why?

What do you remember about your 20s, 30s, 40s, 50s, and 60s? What events stand out in your mind? How was each decade different from the one before it?

There are some ages we don't look forward to. What birthday were you least enthusiastic about? Why?

_____

_____

_____

_____

_____

If you could go back to any age, which age would it be and why?

_____

_____

_____

_____

_____

_____

What was the make, model, and color of your family car?

What was it like growing up with siblings? If you didn't have siblings, what do you think it would have been like if you did?

What did you want most as a child but never got?

_____

_____

_____

_____

_____

Who or what influenced your taste and style as a teenager?

_____

_____

_____

_____

_____

What was the most challenging thing you had to tell your parents as a teenager?

_____

_____

_____

_____

_____

Have you gone through any difficult or stressful situations or times in your life that have taught you valuable lessons? If so, describe the situations and write about what you learned from them.

_____

_____

_____

_____

_____

_____

What was your opinion of college? Did you want to go? If so, where and why?

_____

_____

_____

_____

_____

Did you ever experience peer pressure? What happened, and how did you cope with the situation?

_____

_____

_____

_____

_____

_____

_____

What golden rules do you live by?

What do you know now that you wish you had known when you were young?

What are you most thankful for?

_____

_____

_____

_____

_____

_____

What are you most proud of?

_____

_____

_____

_____

_____

_____

How did you meet the love of your life?

_____

_____

_____

_____

_____

Did you ever experience love at first sight? What happened with this person?

_____

_____

_____

_____

_____

_____

What are the three most significant news events that happened during your lifetime? Why are they important?

What advice did your parents or grandparents give you that you still practice and remember today?

_____

_____

_____

_____

_____

_____

Do your children and grandchildren currently look after you or take care of you? Do you want them to?

_____

_____

_____

_____

_____

Do you think your family is grateful for the impact you have had on their lives?

_____

_____

_____

_____

_____

What does the word "old" mean to you?

_____

_____

_____

_____

_____

Does life seem more complicated now or simpler?

How do you think it will be for future generations?

ADDITIONAL NOTES

About the Author

Katie H. Sweeney is a San Francisco–based journalist and modern-day renaissance woman. She has created captivating and original content for some of the web's leading brands, including *Forbes Travel Guide*, *MyDomaine*, and *PopSugar*. In her spare time, she enjoys crafting delicious meals for her family and friends. One of Katie's favorite people to cook for is her beloved grandfather, Al Hogan. He has taught her to savor the moment and not worry about the past or stress over the future. He says, "If music be the food of love, play on." Learn more about Katie at katiehsweeney.com, and follow her culinary adventures on Instagram at @sweenkatcooks.

CPSIA information can be obtained
at www.ICGtesting.com
Printed in the USA
LVHW071517020820
662193LV00013B/1452